# NEW HORIZONS IN ENGLISH 2
## SECOND EDITION

# WORKBOOK

## LARS MELLGREN
## MICHAEL WALKER

Consulting Editor:
JOHN A. UPSHUR
English Language Institute
University of Michigan

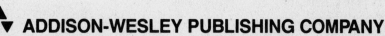
**ADDISON-WESLEY PUBLISHING COMPANY**

Reading, Massachusetts • Menlo Park, California • Don Mills, Ontario
Amsterdam • London • Manila • Singapore • Sydney • Tokyo

Illustrations by Akihito Shirakawa

ISBN 0-201-65014-2
JKLMNOP-WC-8987654

**FIND THE RIGHT WORD**

| 1. | 2. | 3. | 4. |
|---|---|---|---|
| and | brush | friend | is |
| age | bus | from | ice |
| are | boys | for | it's |

| 5. | 6. | 7. | 8. |
|---|---|---|---|
| green | nine | swim | skirt |
| gray | night | sweater | shirt |
| game | nice | small | sport |

| 9. | 10. | 11. | 12. |
|---|---|---|---|
| skate | table | where | with |
| late | theater | when | white |
| skirt | tall | who | wife |

| 13. | 14. | 15. | 16. |
|---|---|---|---|
| pants | right | happy | me |
| pears | read | has | meat |
| parents | red | have | mother |

| 17. | 18. | 19. | 20. |
|---|---|---|---|
| her | floor | man | give |
| hurry | flute | men | girl |
| here | fine | many | go |

| 21. | 22. | 23. | 24. |
|---|---|---|---|
| bed | car | book | far |
| red | cat | boot | car |
| Ted | can | both | are |

**WHAT IS THE WORD?**

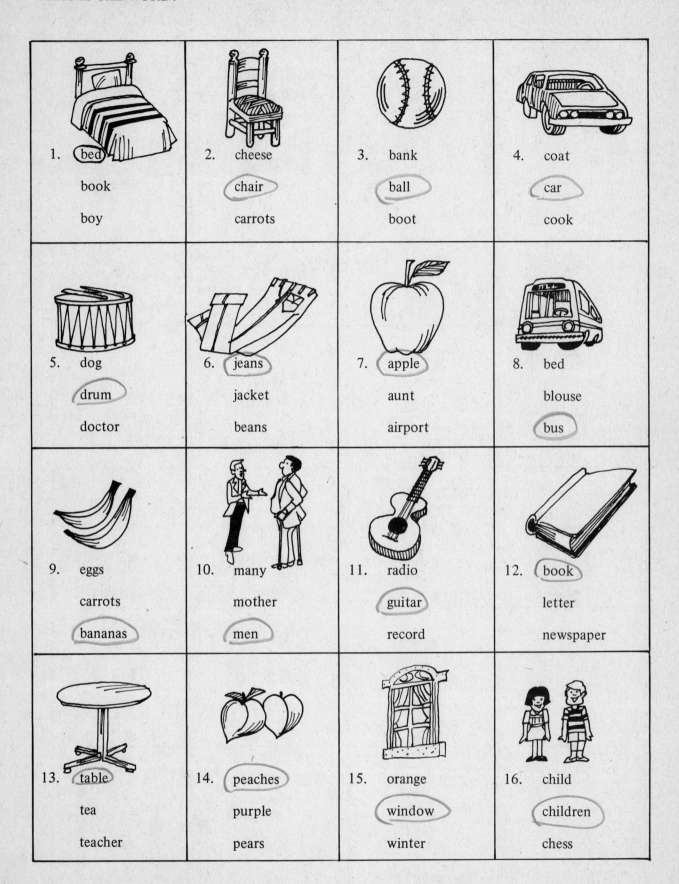

1. (bed)

   book

   boy

2. cheese

   (chair)

   carrots

3. bank

   (ball)

   boot

4. coat

   (car)

   cook

5. dog

   (drum)

   doctor

6. (jeans)

   jacket

   beans

7. (apple)

   aunt

   airport

8. bed

   blouse

   (bus)

9. eggs

   carrots

   (bananas)

10. many

    mother

    (men)

11. radio

    (guitar)

    record

12. (book)

    letter

    newspaper

13. (table)

    tea

    teacher

14. (peaches)

    purple

    pears

15. orange

    (window)

    winter

16. child

    (children)

    chess

**A.** *Read and think carefully as you fill in the blanks.*

1. My . . . . . . . . is Mary Johnson.

2. I'm twenty . . . . . . . . old.

3. I am from Los Angeles.  It is a very big . . . . . . . . .

4. Our house is on Green . . . . . . . .

5. My father is . . . . . . . . accountant.

6. My mother is . . . . . . . . school-bus driver.

7. My brother is . . . . . . . . student.

8. Tom and I are . . . . . . . . to records.

9. My father is . . . . . . . . a football game on T.V.

10. My mother is . . . . . . . . chess.

11. I go . . . . . . . . school every day.

12. There is a football game . . . . . . . . T.V.

13. I am playing cards . . . . . . . . my sister.

14. I have a friend . . . . . . . . . name is Tom.

15. . . . . . . . . . is studying French.

**B.** *Now write about yourself and your family.*

. . . . . . . . . . . . . . . . . . . . . . . . . . . . . . . . . . . . . . . . . . . . . . . . . . . . . . .

. . . . . . . . . . . . . . . . . . . . . . . . . . . . . . . . . . . . . . . . . . . . . . . . . . . . . . .

. . . . . . . . . . . . . . . . . . . . . . . . . . . . . . . . . . . . . . . . . . . . . . . . . . . . . . .

. . . . . . . . . . . . . . . . . . . . . . . . . . . . . . . . . . . . . . . . . . . . . . . . . . . . . . .

. . . . . . . . . . . . . . . . . . . . . . . . . . . . . . . . . . . . . . . . . . . . . . . . . . . . . . .

. . . . . . . . . . . . . . . . . . . . . . . . . . . . . . . . . . . . . . . . . . . . . . . . . . . . . . .

. . . . . . . . . . . . . . . . . . . . . . . . . . . . . . . . . . . . . . . . . . . . . . . . . . . . . . .

. . . . . . . . . . . . . . . . . . . . . . . . . . . . . . . . . . . . . . . . . . . . . . . . . . . . . . .

. . . . . . . . . . . . . . . . . . . . . . . . . . . . . . . . . . . . . . . . . . . . . . . . . . . . . . .

. . . . . . . . . . . . . . . . . . . . . . . . . . . . . . . . . . . . . . . . . . . . . . . . . . . . . . .

## WHAT ARE THEY DOING?

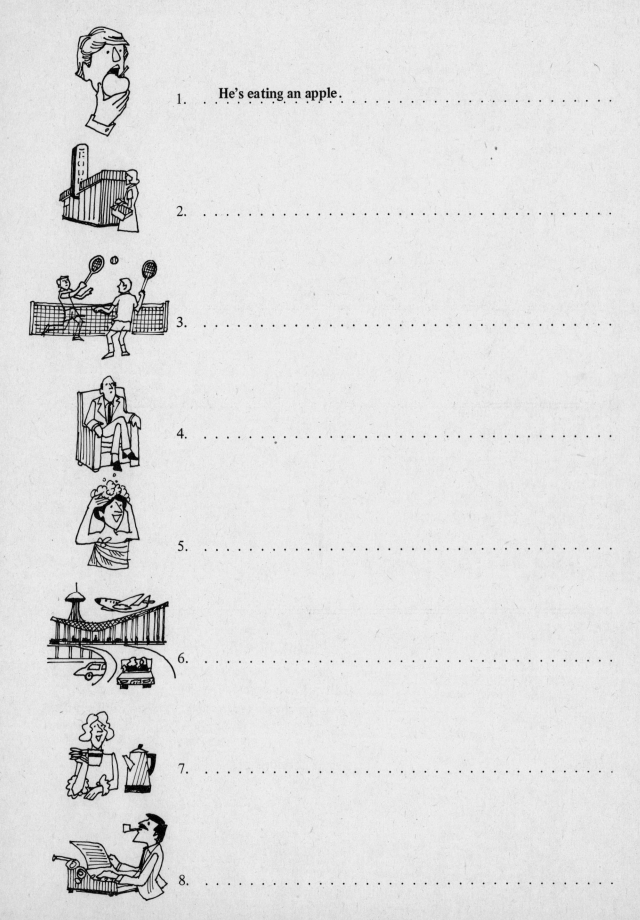

1. He's eating an apple. . . . . . . . . . . . . . . . . . . . . . . . . . . . . . . . . . . . . . .

2. . . . . . . . . . . . . . . . . . . . . . . . . . . . . . . . . . . . . . . . . . . . . . . . . . . . . .

3. . . . . . . . . . . . . . . . . . . . . . . . . . . . . . . . . . . . . . . . . . . . . . . . . . . . . .

4. . . . . . . . . . . . . . . . . . . . . . . . . . . . . . . . . . . . . . . . . . . . . . . . . . . . . .

5. . . . . . . . . . . . . . . . . . . . . . . . . . . . . . . . . . . . . . . . . . . . . . . . . . . . . .

6. . . . . . . . . . . . . . . . . . . . . . . . . . . . . . . . . . . . . . . . . . . . . . . . . . . . . .

7. . . . . . . . . . . . . . . . . . . . . . . . . . . . . . . . . . . . . . . . . . . . . . . . . . . . . .

8. . . . . . . . . . . . . . . . . . . . . . . . . . . . . . . . . . . . . . . . . . . . . . . . . . . . . .

# FIND THE SAME SOUND

**A.**

| | | | | |
|---|---|---|---|---|
| age | take | last | happy | name |
| apple | bad | change | lamp | skate |
| day | late | glad | pants | at |

| GAME | THAT |
|---|---|
| age | apple |
| . . . . . . . . | . . . . . . . . |
| . . . . . . . . | . . . . . . . . |
| . . . . . . . . | . . . . . . . . |

**B.**

| | | | | |
|---|---|---|---|---|
| pen | sleep | meet | well | cheese |
| she | ten | when | bed | chess |
| read | three | we | bread | eggs |

| HE | MEN |
|---|---|
| she | pen |
| . . . . . . . . | . . . . . . . . |
| . . . . . . . . | . . . . . . . . |
| . . . . . . . . | . . . . . . . . |

**C.**

| | | | | |
|---|---|---|---|---|
| bridge | drive | it | him | sing |
| child | fish | ice | hi | still |
| in | five | night | nice | white |

| TIE | THIN |
|---|---|
| child | bridge |
| . . . . . . . . | . . . . . . . . |
| . . . . . . . . | . . . . . . . . |
| . . . . . . . . | . . . . . . . . |

**YES OR NO?**

An apple is red.

| | YES | NO |
|---|---|---|
| | ✓ | |

1. Carrots play the drums.
2. A teacher drives a bus.
3. At noon is 2:00.
4. Bananas are purple.
5. Many dogs are brown.

| | YES | NO |
|---|---|---|
| | | |

6. You can drink fish.
7. Some women are tall.
8. You can eat chess.
9. Children have two eyes.
10. Blond hair is yellow.

**WHAT'S THE WORD?**

A  helps people. ....doctor....

1. He's eating a  . ...........

2. These  are chubby. ...........

3. These  are new. ...........

4. He can play  . ...........

5. Father drives the car to the  . ...........

6. There are many books in the  . ...........

7. There are two  here. ...........

6

Review

**WHAT DO YOU WANT TO DO?**

A.

What do you want to play? . . . . . . . . . . . . . I want to play tennis. . . . . . . . . . . . . . .

1. What do you want to drink? . . . . . . . . . . . . . . . . . . . . . . . . . . . . . . . . . .

2. What do you want to paint? . . . . . . . . . . . . . . . . . . . . . . . . . . . . . . . . . .

3. What do you want to eat? . . . . . . . . . . . . . . . . . . . . . . . . . . . . . . . . . .

4. What do you want to wear? . . . . . . . . . . . . . . . . . . . . . . . . . . . . . . . . . .

5. What do you want to read? . . . . . . . . . . . . . . . . . . . . . . . . . . . . . . . . . .

6. What do you want to play? . . . . . . . . . . . . . . . . . . . . . . . . . . . . . . . . . .

B.

Do you want to play tennis? . . . . . . . No, I want to play chess. . . . . . . . . . . . . . .

1. Do they want to eat fish? . . . . . . . . . . . . . . . . . . . . . . . . . . . . . . . . . .

2. Do you want to play the guitar? . . . . . . . . . . . . . . . . . . . . . . . . . . . . . . . .

3. Do you want to clean the windows? . . . . . . . . . . . . . . . . . . . . . . . . . . . . . . .

4. Do they want to play checkers? . . . . . . . . . . . . . . . . . . . . . . . . . . . . . . . .

5. Do they want to drink lemonade? . . . . . . . . . . . . . . . . . . . . . . . . . . . . . . . .

6. Do you want to read a book? . . . . . . . . . . . . . . . . . . . . . . . . . . . . . . . . . .

**WHAT'S IN THERE?**

**A.**

What do you have?      **I have a box.** . . . . . . . . . . . . . . . . . . . . . . . . . . .

1. What do they have?      **They have a guitar.** . . . . . . . . . . . . . . . . . . . . .

2. What do they have? . . . . . . . . . . . . . . . . . . . . . . . . . . . . . . . . . . . . . . . . . . . . . . . . .

3. What do you have? . . . . . . . . . . . . . . . . . . . . . . . . . . . . . . . . . . . . . . . . . . . . . . . . .

4. What do they have? . . . . . . . . . . . . . . . . . . . . . . . . . . . . . . . . . . . . . . . . . . . . . . . . .

5. What do you have? . . . . . . . . . . . . . . . . . . . . . . . . . . . . . . . . . . . . . . . . . . . . . . . . .

6. What do we have? . . . . . . . . . . . . . . . . . . . . . . . . . . . . . . . . . . . . . . . . . . . . . . . . .

**B.**

Do you have a cat in there?      **No, I have a dog.** . . . . . . . . . . . . . . . . . . .

1. Do you have a football in there? . . . . . . . . . . . . . . . . . . . . . . . . . . . . . . . . . . . . . . .

2. Do you have a dress in there? . . . . . . . . . . . . . . . . . . . . . . . . . . . . . . . . . . . . . . . . .

3. Do you have a pineapple in there? . . . . . . . . . . . . . . . . . . . . . . . . . . . . . . . . . . . . .

4. Do you have a guitar in there? . . . . . . . . . . . . . . . . . . . . . . . . . . . . . . . . . . . . . . . .

5. Do you have a ball in there? . . . . . . . . . . . . . . . . . . . . . . . . . . . . . . . . . . . . . . . . . .

6. Do you have a fish in there? . . . . . . . . . . . . . . . . . . . . . . . . . . . . . . . . . . . . . . . . . .

**WHEN? HOW? WHERE?**

**How are you going?** . . . . . . . . . . . . . . . . . . . . . . . . . **By bus.**

1. . . . . . . . . . . . . . . . . . . . . . . . . . . . . . . At midnight.

2. . . . . . . . . . . . . . . . . . . . . . . . . . . . . By motorcycle.

3. . . . . . . . . . . . . . . . . . . . . . . . . . . . . To the theater.

4. . . . . . . . . . . . . . . . . . . . . . . . . . . . . At noon.

5. . . . . . . . . . . . . . . . . . . . . . . . . . . . . By car.

6. . . . . . . . . . . . . . . . . . . . . . . . . . . . . To the disco.

7. . . . . . . . . . . . . . . . . . . . . . . . . . . . . At five thirty.

8. . . . . . . . . . . . . . . . . . . . . . . . . . . . . To the bus station.

## ODD MAN OUT

**garages, churches, schools, sweaters, banks** . . . sweaters . . . . . .

1. swimming, dancing, skating, drizzling, singing . . . . . . . . . . . .

2. nurse, secretary, doctor, student, rug . . . . . . . . . . . .

3. on, water, under, behind, in front of . . . . . . . . . . . .

4. purple, yellow, yard, green, red . . . . . . . . . . .

5. midnight, party, noon, morning, evening . . . . . . . . . . .

6. him, us, her, their, them . . . . . . . . . . .

7. uncle, sister, aunt, cousin . . . . . . . . . . .

1. When does Mrs. Brown eat breakfast?

   **She eats breakfast at 8.**
   . . . . . . . . . . . . . . . . . . . . . . . . . . . . . . . . . . . . . . . . . . . . .

2. When does she wash the clothes?

   . . . . . . . . . . . . . . . . . . . . . . . . . . . . . . . . . . . . . . . . . . . . .

3. What does she do at 9?

   . . . . . . . . . . . . . . . . . . . . . . . . . . . . . . . . . . . . . . . . . . . . .

4. When does she clean the house?

   . . . . . . . . . . . . . . . . . . . . . . . . . . . . . . . . . . . . . . . . . . . . .

5. What does she do at 7?

   . . . . . . . . . . . . . . . . . . . . . . . . . . . . . . . . . . . . . . . . . . . . .

6. When does she write letters?

   . . . . . . . . . . . . . . . . . . . . . . . . . . . . . . . . . . . . . . . . . . . . .

7. When does she play tennis?

   . . . . . . . . . . . . . . . . . . . . . . . . . . . . . . . . . . . . . . . . . . . . .

8. What does she do at 11?

   . . . . . . . . . . . . . . . . . . . . . . . . . . . . . . . . . . . . . . . . . . . . .

# WHAT DO THEY DO?

**A.** What does a taxi driver do? · · · · · · · **He drives a taxi.** · · · · · · · · · · · ·

1. What does a singer do? · · · · · · · · · · · · · · · · · · · · · · · · · · · · ·

2. What does a chef do? · · · · · · · · · · · · · · · · · · · · · · · · · · · · ·

3. What does a newspaper boy do? · · · · · · · · · · · · · · · · · · · · · · · · · · · · ·

4. What does a writer do? · · · · · · · · · · · · · · · · · · · · · · · · · · · · ·

5. What does a football player do? · · · · · · · · · · · · · · · · · · · · · · · · · · · · ·

**B.** **What's this woman?**      **She's a tennis player.** · · · · · ·

     **What does she do for a living?**      **She plays tennis.** · · · · · · · · ·

1. What's this man? · · · · · · · · · · · · · · · · · · · · · · · · · · · · ·

     What does he do for a living? · · · · · · · · · · · · · · · · · · · · · · · · · · · · ·

2. What's this man? · · · · · · · · · · · · · · · · · · · · · · · · · · · · ·

     What does he do for a living? · · · · · · · · · · · · · · · · · · · · · · · · · · · · ·

3. What's this woman? · · · · · · · · · · · · · · · · · · · · · · · · · · · · ·

     What does she do for a living? · · · · · · · · · · · · · · · · · · · · · · · · · · · · ·

4. What's this man? · · · · · · · · · · · · · · · · · · · · · · · · · · · · ·

     What does he do for a living? · · · · · · · · · · · · · · · · · · · · · · · · · · · · ·

5. What's this woman? · · · · · · · · · · · · · · · · · · · · · · · · · · · · ·

     What does she do for a living? · · · · · · · · · · · · · · · · · · · · · · · · · · · · ·

## WHAT ARE THEY DOING NOW?

**He likes to ski.** . . . . . . . . . . . . . . **He's skiing now.** . . . . . . . . . . . . . . Unit Two

1. She likes to swim. . . . . . . . . . . . . . . . . . . . . . . . . . . . . . . . . .

2. He likes to cook. . . . . . . . . . . . . . . . . . . . . . . . . . . . . . . . . .

3. They like to play tennis. . . . . . . . . . . . . . . . . . . . . . . . . . . . . .

4. She likes to eat. . . . . . . . . . . . . . . . . . . . . . . . . . . . . . . . . .

5. He likes to skate. . . . . . . . . . . . . . . . . . . . . . . . . . . . . . . . . .

6. He likes to dance. . . . . . . . . . . . . . . . . . . . . . . . . . . . . . . . . .

7. They like to sing. . . . . . . . . . . . . . . . . . . . . . . . . . . . . . . . . .

8. They like to go to the theater. . . . . . . . . . . . . . . . . . . . . . . . . . .

9. He likes to ride horses. . . . . . . . . . . . . . . . . . . . . . . . . . . . . . .

10. She likes to go to the store. . . . . . . . . . . . . . . . . . . . . . . . . . . .

## HOW MANY ARE WORDS?

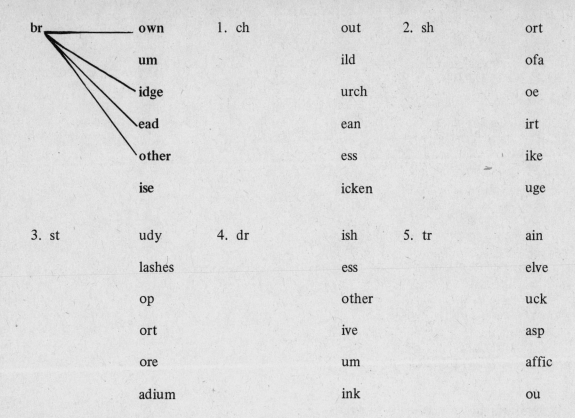

| br | | 1. ch | | 2. sh | |
|----|------|-------|-------|-------|------|
| | own | | out | | ort |
| | um | | ild | | ofa |
| | idge | | urch | | oe |
| | ead | | ean | | irt |
| | other | | ess | | ike |
| | ise | | icken | | uge |

| 3. st | | 4. dr | | 5. tr | |
|-------|--------|-------|-------|-------|-------|
| | udy | | ish | | ain |
| | lashes | | ess | | elve |
| | op | | other | | uck |
| | ort | | ive | | asp |
| | ore | | um | | affic |
| | adium | | ink | | ou |

## WHAT'S THE RIGHT WORD?

You wear this on your foot.    **s h o e**

1. Not tall.    — — — — —

2. A color.    — — — — —

3. A game to play.    — — — — —

4. You can drive this.    — — — — —

5. You can eat this.    — — — — —

6. An instrument.    — — — —

7. You can ride on it.    — — — — —

8. A girl wears this.    — — — — —

**YES OR NO?**

A blouse can sing.      . . no . . . . . . .

Blue is a color.      . . yes . . . . . . .

1.  A rug can shave.      . . . . . . . . . . . . . . .

2.  A house has windows.      . . . . . . . . . . . . . .

3.  Peter is a boy's name.      . . . . . . . . . . . . . .

4.  Books are good to drink.      . . . . . . . . . . . . . .

5.  A dog can cook breakfast.      . . . . . . . . . . . . .

6.  You can listen to records.      . . . . . . . . . . . . .

7.  You can buy peaches at the post office.      . . . . . . . . . . . . .

8.  You can buy bread at the supermarket.      . . . . . . . . . . . . .

9.  You often see cats dancing.      . . . . . . . . . . . . .

10.  A tennis player plays with a racket.      . . . . . . . . . . . . .

11.  A lazy man doesn't like to go to sleep.      . . . . . . . . . . . .

12.  Both boys and girls wear jeans.      . . . . . . . . . . . .

13.  Both boys and girls wear carrots.      . . . . . . . . . . . . .

14.  Many boys can play the guitar.      . . . . . . . . . . . .

15.  A train goes to the bus stop.      . . . . . . . . . . . .

16.  You often wear pajamas to the theater.      . . . . . . . . . . .

17.  Peaches can walk.      . . . . . . . . . . . . .

18.  You play checkers with 52 cards.      . . . . . . . . . . . . .

**WHAT ARE THEY DOING?**

What's that boy doing?  He's . . . playing chess. . . . . . . . . . . . . . .

Does he . . play. . . . . . . . . . every day?  No, . . but he's playing now. . . . . .

1. What's that girl doing?  She's . . . . . . . . . . . . . . . . . . . . .

   Does she . . . . . . . . . every day?  No, . . . . . . . . . . . . . . . . . . .

2. What's that man doing?  He's . . . . . . . . . . . . . . . . . . . . .

   Does he . . . . . . . . every day?  . . . . . . . . . . . . . . . . . . . .

3. What's that woman doing?  . . . . . . . . . . . . . . . . . . . . .

   . . . . . . . . . . . . . . every day?  . . . . . . . . . . . . . . . . . . . .

4. What's that boy doing?  . . . . . . . . . . . . . . . . . . . . .

   . . . . . . . . . . . . . . . . .  . . . . . . . . . . . . . . . . . . . .

5. What's that man doing?  . . . . . . . . . . . . . . . . . . . . .

   Does he . . . . . . . . milk every day?  . . . . . . . . . . . . . . . . . . . .

6. What's this woman doing?  . . . . . . . . . . . . . . . . . . . . .

   Does . . . . . . . . every day?  . . . . . . . . . . . . . . . . . . . .

7. What's this girl doing?  . . . . . . . . . . . . . . . . . . . . .

   . . . . . . . . . . . . . . . . .  . . . . . . . . . . . . . . . . . . . .

**A.**

**How often do you . . .**

| | Always | Sometimes | Seldom | Never |
|---|---|---|---|---|
| 1. wash your hands? | | ✓ | | |
| 2. eat breakfast? | | | | |
| 3. go to the library? | | | | |
| 4. buy a sandwich? | | | | |
| 5. talk too much? | | | | |
| 6. get up at six? | | | | |
| 7. go to bed at eight? | | | | |
| 8. cook dinner? | | | | |
| 9. study? | | | | |
| 10. help in the house? | | | | |

**B.**

1. Do you always eat breakfast?

    **Yes, I always do./No, I never do.**
. . . . . . . . . . . . . . . . . . . . . . . . . . . . . . . . . . . . . . . . . . . . . . . . . . . .

2. Do you frequently go to the movies?

. . . . . . . . . . . . . . . . . . . . . . . . . . . . . . . . . . . . . . . . . . . . . . . . . . . .

3. Do you sometimes have eggs for breakfast?

. . . . . . . . . . . . . . . . . . . . . . . . . . . . . . . . . . . . . . . . . . . . . . . . . . . .

4. Do you always watch T.V. at night?

. . . . . . . . . . . . . . . . . . . . . . . . . . . . . . . . . . . . . . . . . . . . . . . . . . . .

5. Do you usually cook dinner?

. . . . . . . . . . . . . . . . . . . . . . . . . . . . . . . . . . . . . . . . . . . . . . . . . . . .

6. Do you frequently study with a friend?

. . . . . . . . . . . . . . . . . . . . . . . . . . . . . . . . . . . . . . . . . . . . . . . . . . . .

7. Do you always sleep all afternoon?

. . . . . . . . . . . . . . . . . . . . . . . . . . . . . . . . . . . . . . . . . . . . . . . . . . . .

**HOW MANY ARE WORDS?**

1.  pai                      2.  pru

    fra                          cru

    aw                          ba

    dea         nt              cha          nk

    pare                      trai

    wa                         tha

    stude                    dri

3.  bla                      4.  pea

    loo                        chur

    so                         tow

    ple         ck              tea          ch

    tru                        cha

    clo                        che

    gla                        wat

5.  bea                      6.  co

    fi                           dar

    cat                        stu

    wa         sh              jw          st

    sli                        la

    poli                      sla

    bru                      pa

I buy . . .my. . . . . lunch every day.

He buys . . .his. . . . . lunch often.

1. She washes . . . . . . . . . car every week.

2. They cook . . . . . . . . . dinner.

3. Did you get . . . . . . . . mail?

4. Does she see . . . . . . . . . friend often?

5. I always study . . . . . . . . book.

6. Are you leaving . . . . . . . . new hat here?

7. We can't find . . . . . . . . coats.

8. She seldom drives . . . . . . . . car.

9. Bob and I are playing . . . . . . . . records.

10. He is wearing . . . . . . . . jacket.

11. Mother is looking for . . . . . . . . brush.

12. The Browns are having . . . . . . . . party tomorrow.

13. Susan is taking . . . . . . . . vacation in January.

14. My brother likes to paint . . . . . . . . room.

15. Bob and I cook . . . . . . . . lunches frequently.

16. Frank and Dick have . . . . . . . . parents' car.

17. I want . . . . . . . . ice cream now.

18. Do you want to eat . . . . . . . . dinner now?

## HOW DO THEY SOUND?

| | | | | |
|---|---|---|---|---|
| eats | arrives | shaves | speaks | comes |
| drinks | chases | cleans | works | lifts |
| writes | dances | hurries | splashes | helps |
| washes | walks | dries | kisses | teaches |
| brushes | sleeps | costs | runs | finds |

| GET[S] | SWIMS[Z] | CHANGES[IZ] |
|---|---|---|
| eats | arrives | washes |
| | | |
| | | |
| | | |
| | | |
| | | |
| | | |
| | | |
| | | |
| | | |

**She is brushing her hair.**       **She brushes it every day.**

**She is playing tennis.**       **She plays tennis every day.**

1.  The girl is hurrying.    . . . . . . . . . . . . . . . . . . . .

2.  He is emptying the trash.   . . . . . . . . . . . . . . . . . .

3.  She is drying her hands.   . . . . . . . . . . . . . . . . . .

4.  . . . . . . . . . . . . . . . . . . .   He teaches every day.

5.  . . . . . . . . . . . . . . . . . .   The plane flies every day.

6.  . . . . . . . . . . . . . . . . . .   He carries his lunch every day.

7.  She is kissing the baby.   . . . . . . . . . . . . . . . . . . . .

8.  He is working.   . . . . . . . . . . . . . . . . . . . .

9.  She is trying to study.   . . . . . . . . . . . . . . . . . . . .

10. She is watching T.V.   . . . . . . . . . . . . . . . . . . . .

11. . . . . . . . . . . . . . . . . . .   He takes a shower every day.

12. . . . . . . . . . . . . . . . . . .   She washes her hair every day.

13. . . . . . . . . . . . . . . . . . .   He hurries to the bus every day.

14. He is delivering mail.   . . . . . . . . . . . . . . . . . . . .

15. She is carrying the baby.   . . . . . . . . . . . . . . . . . . . .

**WASH**

    He - face                 **He washes his face.** . . . . . . . . . . . . . . . .

    1. You - face               . . . . . . . . . . . . . . . . . . . . . . . .

    2. They - shirts            . . . . . . . . . . . . . . . . . . . . . . . .

    3. She - blouse            . . . . . . . . . . . . . . . . . . . . . . . .

    4. We - car                . . . . . . . . . . . . . . . . . . . . . . . .

    5. I - sweater             . . . . . . . . . . . . . . . . . . . . . . . .

    6. He - windows           . . . . . . . . . . . . . . . . . . . . . . . .

**CARRY**

    Tom - bag                **Tom carries his bag.** . . . . . . . . . . . . . . . .

    1. Father - book           . . . . . . . . . . . . . . . . . . . . . . . .

    2. Lucy - guitar            . . . . . . . . . . . . . . . . . . . . . . . .

    3. Don - football          . . . . . . . . . . . . . . . . . . . . . . . .

    4. I - paddle              . . . . . . . . . . . . . . . . . . . . . . . .

    5. Mother - baggage       . . . . . . . . . . . . . . . . . . . . . . . .

**DRY**

    Don - hair               **Don dries his hair.** . . . . . . . . . . . . . . . .

    1. Sue - clothes           . . . . . . . . . . . . . . . . . . . . . . . .

    2. Mother - hands         . . . . . . . . . . . . . . . . . . . . . . . .

    3. I - dog                 . . . . . . . . . . . . . . . . . . . . . . . .

    4. Jack - raincoat         . . . . . . . . . . . . . . . . . . . . . . . .

## WHAT'S THE RIGHT WORD?

Chess / **Cheese** **is good to eat.**

1. A boy seldom wears a    skirt. / **shirt**

2. What is your last    game? / **name?**

3. What color is his    **hair?** / here?

4. How do you    **like** / look    my new dress?

5. Do you brush your    teach / **teeth**    every day?

6. Are you    **still** / stand    a student?

7. I'm    **fine.** / funny.    How are you?

8. Do you swim    evening / **every**    day?

9. Are you leaving    new? / **now?**

10. Please    talk / **walk**    to the bus stop.

# FIND THE RIGHT WORD

| | | | |
|---|---|---|---|
| 1. run<br>rug<br>ring | 2. clothes<br>cloudy<br>clean | 3. sit<br>city<br>ski | 4. have<br>hat<br>hand |
| 5. to<br>new<br>shoe | 6. lunch<br>last<br>lamp | 7. changes<br>chases<br>crashes | 8. snow<br>know<br>now |
| 9. smoke<br>splash<br>speak | 10. take<br>ask<br>makes | 11. shoes<br>shorts<br>she | 12. ball<br>tall<br>all |
| 13. doesn't<br>does<br>do | 14. cheese<br>chess<br>chair | 15. first<br>from<br>friend | 16. puddles<br>paddles<br>parents |
| 17. hotel<br>home<br>hope | 18. never<br>every<br>ever | 19. talk<br>truck<br>try | 20. carries<br>hurries<br>helps |
| 21. bank<br>thank<br>that | 22. fly<br>friend<br>fine | 23. boyfriend<br>girl friend<br>friend | 24. where<br>what<br>water |

**WHERE?  WHEN?  HOW?**

1. Where is John going?  **He's going to school.** . . . . . . . . . . . . . . . . . . . .

2. Where are Sue and Don going? . . . . . . . . . . . . . . . . . . . . . . . . .

3. Where are your parents going? . . . . . . . . . . . . . . . . . . . . . . . . .

4. Where are you going? . . . . . . . . . . . . . . . . . . . . . . . . . . . . . .

5. When are you going? . . . . . . . . . . . . . . . . . . . . . . . . . . . . . .

6. When is John going? . . . . . . . . . . . . . . . . . . . . . . . . . . . . . .

7. When are the Browns going? . . . . . . . . . . . . . . . . . . . . . . . . .

8. How are they going? . . . . . . . . . . . . . . . . . . . . . . . . . . . . . .

9. How is he going? . . . . . . . . . . . . . . . . . . . . . . . . . . . . . . . .

10. How are you going? . . . . . . . . . . . . . . . . . . . . . . . . . . . . . .

# WHAT ARE THEY GOING TO DO?

A.     What's she going to do?                      **She's going to read a book.** . . . . . . .

1.   What's he going to do?                       . . . . . . . . . . . . . . . . . . .

2.   What's she going to do?                    . . . . . . . . . . . . . . . . . . .

3.   What are they going to do?                 . . . . . . . . . . . . . . . . . . .

4.   What's it going to do?                     . . . . . . . . . . . . . . . . . . .

5.   What's he going to do?                     . . . . . . . . . . . . . . . . . . .

B.     Is she going to read?                       **No, she's going to drive a car.**

1.   Is she going to sing?                      . . . . . . . . . . . . . . . . . . .

2.   Are they going to play tennis?             . . . . . . . . . . . . . . . . . . .

3.   Is he going to drive?                      . . . . . . . . . . . . . . . . . . .

4.   Are they going to watch TV?               . . . . . . . . . . . . . . . . . . .

5.   Is he going to ski?                        . . . . . . . . . . . . . . . . . . .

## WHAT ARE THEY GOING TO DO?

Dan has a newspaper.                    He's going to read. . . . . . . . . . . . . . . . .

Jane has a pen and paper.              . She's going to write. . . . . . . . . . . . . . . .

1. Don is walking to the pool.          . . . . . . . . . . . . . . . . . . . . . . . . .

2. John and Jack have rackets.          . . . . . . . . . . . . . . . . . . . . . . . . .

3. Mary is looking at her dirty car.    . . . . . . . . . . . . . . . . . . . . . . . . .

4. The dog is hungry.                   . . . . . . . . . . . . . . . . . . . . . . . . .

5. Judy is very tired.                  . . . . . . . . . . . . . . . . . . . . . . . . .

6. Sam is looking at his records.       . . . . . . . . . . . . . . . . . . . . . . . . .

7. Mrs. Brown is looking at a dirty window.   . . . . . . . . . . . . . . . . . . . . . .

8. Sue is asleep. The alarm clock rings.      . . . . . . . . . . . . . . . . . . . . . .

9. Bill sits down in front of the T.V.   . . . . . . . . . . . . . . . . . . . . . . . .

10. June and Bob have their chess game.  . . . . . . . . . . . . . . . . . . . . . . . .

11. Robert sits down at the piano.       . . . . . . . . . . . . . . . . . . . . . . . .

12. Mary is sitting at her typewriter.   . . . . . . . . . . . . . . . . . . . . . . . .

# WHICH STORIES TELL ABOUT THE PICTURES?

1.      2.      3.

. . . . . .    Mary is going to bed. She is wearing her pajamas. She is going to read a book after she drinks her milk. On the table by her bed are a lamp, a glass of milk, and an alarm clock.

. . . . . .    Mary is going to bed. She is wearing her pajamas. She is going to read a book after she drinks her milk. On the table by her bed are a lamp, a glass of milk, and flowers.

. . . . . .    Tom is going to a rock concert. He's wearing a funny hat, a blue shirt, his jeans, and his boots. He is going to put on a jacket or a sweater.

. . . . . .    Tom is going to a rock concert. He's wearing a blue shirt, his jeans, and his boots. He is going to put on a jacket or a sweater.

. . . . . .    A movie star is sitting by a pool. Three photographers are taking her picture. She is wearing a dress and a big hat. She is smoking.

. . . . . .    A movie star is sitting by a pool. Three photographers are taking her picture. She is wearing a bathing suit and sunglasses. She is smoking.

**BRUSH**

He . . brushes . . . . . . . . his teeth every day.

He . . is brushing . . . . . his teeth now.

He . 's going to brush . . . . . . . . his teeth tomorrow.

1. HURRY

She . . . . . . . . . . . . to work every day.

She . . . . . . . . . . . now.

She . . . . . . . . . . . . . . . tomorrow.

2. DRIVE

Father . . . . . . . . . . . now.

He . . . . . . . . . . . . . . . tomorrow.

He . . . . . . . . . . . . every day.

3. WATCH

Mother often . . . . . . . . . . . T.V.

She . . . . . . . . . . . . it now.

She . . . . . . . . . . . . . . . . it tonight.

4. STUDY

Tom . . . . . . . . . . . . . . . tomorrow.

He never . . . . . . . . . . . . on Tuesday.

He . . . . . . . . . . . now.

**Do you like apples?**  . . . . . . . . **Yes, I do.** . . . . . . . .

1. Does he like to ski? . . . . . . . . . . . . . . . . . . . .

2. Do you like carrots? . . . . . . . . . . . . . . . . . . . .

3. Does she like fish? . . . . . . . . . . . . . . . . . . . .

4. Do they like to eat? . . . . . . . . . . . . . . . . . . . .

5. Does he like to study? . . . . . . . . . . . . . . . . . . .

6. Do you like chicken? . . . . . . . . . . . . . . . . . . . .

7. Does he like to drive? . . . . . . . . . . . . . . . . . . .

8. Does she like lettuce? . . . . . . . . . . . . . . . . . . .

9. Does he like Sue? . . . . . . . . . . . . . . . . . . . .

10. Does Sue like him? . . . . . . . . . . . . . . . . . . .

11. Do you like to skate? . . . . . . . . . . . . . . . . . . .

1. Did you drink your milk?                 No, I didn't. . . . . . . . . . . . . . . . . . . .

2. Did he eat?                              . . . . . . . . . . . . . . . . . . . . . . . . . .

3. Did he drive his car?                    . . . . . . . . . . . . . . . . . . . . . . . . . .

4. Did she wax her car?                     . . . . . . . . . . . . . . . . . . . . . . . . . .

5. Did he put on his shoes?                 . . . . . . . . . . . . . . . . . . . . . . . . . .

6. Did they take a taxi?                    . . . . . . . . . . . . . . . . . . . . . . . . . .

7. Did you drink coffee?                    . . . . . . . . . . . . . . . . . . . . . . . . . .

8. Did she study at seven?                  . . . . . . . . . . . . . . . . . . . . . . . . . .

9. Did you close the window?                . . . . . . . . . . . . . . . . . . . . . . . . . .

10. Did they go to the store?               . . . . . . . . . . . . . . . . . . . . . . . . . .

## QUESTIONS AND ANSWERS

**When did you clean your room?**    (yesterday)

   **I cleaned it yesterday.**
. . . . . . . . . . . . . . . . . . . . . . . . . . . . . . . .


**Who did she marry?**    (Tom)

   **She married Tom.**
. . . . . . . . . . . . . . . . . . . . . . . . . . . . . . . .


1. When did you listen to records?    (yesterday)

. . . . . . . . . . . . . . . . . . . . . . . . . . . . . . . .

2. What did you pick up at the station?    (my tickets)

. . . . . . . . . . . . . . . . . . . . . . . . . . . . . . . .

3. What did you paint yesterday?    (the house)

. . . . . . . . . . . . . . . . . . . . . . . . . . . . . . . .

4. When did he wash the dishes?    (this morning)

. . . . . . . . . . . . . . . . . . . . . . . . . . . . . . . .

5. Did you talk to Jack or Tom?    (Tom)

. . . . . . . . . . . . . . . . . . . . . . . . . . . . . . . .

6. When did you play tennis?    (last week)

. . . . . . . . . . . . . . . . . . . . . . . . . . . . . . . .

7. What did you carry?    (Mary's books)

. . . . . . . . . . . . . . . . . . . . . . . . . . . . . . . .

8. What did they play yesterday?    (tennis)

. . . . . . . . . . . . . . . . . . . . . . . . . . . . . . . .

**WHAT DID THEY DO?**

**What did he paint?**     **He painted the window.** . . . . . . . . . . . . . . . .

1. What did she close?     . . . . . . . . . . . . . . . . . . . . . . . . . . . . . . . .

2. When did they arrive?     . . . . . . . . . . . . . . . . . . . . . . . . . . . . . . . .

3. What did she wash?     . . . . . . . . . . . . . . . . . . . . . . . . . . . . . . . .

4. What did she bake?     . . . . . . . . . . . . . . . . . . . . . . . . . . . . . . . .

5. What did they carry?     . . . . . . . . . . . . . . . . . . . . . . . . . . . . . . . .

6. What did she dry?     . . . . . . . . . . . . . . . . . . . . . . . . . . . . . . . .

7. What did you open?     . . . . . . . . . . . . . . . . . . . . . . . . . . . . . . . .

8. What did he wax?     . . . . . . . . . . . . . . . . . . . . . . . . . . . . . . . .

9. When did they play?     . . . . . . . . . . . . . . . . . . . . . . . . . . . . . . . .

10. What did she open?     . . . . . . . . . . . . . . . . . . . . . . . . . . . . . . . .

11. What did they fry?     . . . . . . . . . . . . . . . . . . . . . . . . . . . . . . . .

12. What did she brush?     . . . . . . . . . . . . . . . . . . . . . . . . . . . . . . . .

13. What did she plant?     . . . . . . . . . . . . . . . . . . . . . . . . . . . . . . . .

14. What did you miss?     . . . . . . . . . . . . . . . . . . . . . . . . . . . . . . . .

## WHAT DID THEY DO?

**Did they arrive at nine?**

No, they didn't arrive at nine. . . . . . . . .

They arrived at ten. . . . . . . . . . . . . . . . . . . . . . . .

1. Did he close the window?

. . . . . . . . . . . . . . . . . . . . . . . . . . . . . . . . . . . . . . . .

. . . . . . . . . . . . . . . . . . . . . . . . . . . . . . . . . . . . . . . .

2. Did they return at midnight?

. . . . . . . . . . . . . . . . . . . . . . . . . . . . . . . . . . . . . . . .

. . . . . . . . . . . . . . . . . . . . . . . . . . . . . . . . . . . . . . . .

3. Did she paint the gate?

. . . . . . . . . . . . . . . . . . . . . . . . . . . . . . . . . . . . . . . .

. . . . . . . . . . . . . . . . . . . . . . . . . . . . . . . . . . . . . . . .

4. Did they want an apartment?

. . . . . . . . . . . . . . . . . . . . . . . . . . . . . . . . . . . . . . . .

. . . . . . . . . . . . . . . . . . . . . . . . . . . . . . . . . . . . . . . .

5. Did you rent a car?

. . . . . . . . . . . . . . . . . . . . . . . . . . . . . . . . . . . . . . . .

. . . . . . . . . . . . . . . . . . . . . . . . . . . . . . . . . . . . . . . .

6. Did she clean the living room?

. . . . . . . . . . . . . . . . . . . . . . . . . . . . . . . . . . . . . . . .

## WHAT SOUND IS THIS?

| | -D | -T | -ID |
|---|---|---|---|
| 1. I picked up the book. | | X | |
| 2. Jerry painted his house. | | | |
| 3. I talked to Mary. | | | |
| 4. We played tennis today. | | | |
| 5. He hurried to school. | | | |
| 6. They polished their shoes. | | | |
| 7. I washed the clothes. | | | |
| 8. She carried the box. | | | |
| 9. They copied the music. | | | |
| 10. He waited at the bus stop. | | | |

**USE THE RIGHT WORD**

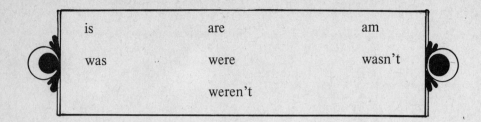

| is | are | am |
| was | were | wasn't |
| | weren't | |

1.  My brother stayed in bed yesterday. He . . . **wasn't** . . . . sailing with us.

2.  Sue . . . is . . . . . playing the piano.

3.  They . were . . swimming in the pool yesterday.

4.  Were . . . . you watching the game last night?

5.  They didn't eat dinner. They . weren't . very hungry.

6.  Bob . was . . . in London last week.

7.  I . was . . . very tired.

8.  Was . . . Betty with you this morning? No, she . . . . . . . .

9.  Tim . . is . . . . going to play tennis now.

10. Sue and Sally . were . . very late yesterday.

11. Mother . . was . . cooking dinner when I arrived.

12. Are . . . . you still a student?

13. The boys . was . . . late yesterday, but they . are . . . early today.

14. Father . . . is . . . . very tall.

15. I can't talk now. I . am . . . doing my homework.

# WHAT ARE THEY DOING?

ACROSS

DOWN

**FIND THE REAL WORD**

A.

1. sloec   **close** . . . . . . . . . .      9. niro   . . . . . . . . . . . . . .

2. eabk   . . . . . . . . . .      10. trie   . . . . . . . . . . . . . .

3. seey   *eyes* . . . . . .      11. rmsa   . . . . . . . . . . . . . .

4. gles   *legs* . . . . . .      12. vaew   . . . . . . . . . . . . . .

5. ubnr   . . . . . . . . . .      13. skisde   . . . . . . . . . . . . .

6. lenoa   . . . . . . . . . .      14. npita   . . . . . . . . . . . . .

7. veor   . . . . . . . . . .      15. sdser   . . . . . . . . . . . . .

8. sllwa   . . . . . . . . . .      16. gigjong   . . . . . . . . . . . .

B.

Now use some of the words in good sentences.

1. . . . . . . . . . . . . . . . . . . . . . . . . . . . . . . . . . . . . . . . . .

2. . . . . . . . . . . . . . . . . . . . . . . . . . . . . . . . . . . . . . . . . .

3. . . . . . . . . . . . . . . . . . . . . . . . . . . . . . . . . . . . . . . . . .

4. . . . . . . . . . . . . . . . . . . . . . . . . . . . . . . . . . . . . . . . . .

5. . . . . . . . . . . . . . . . . . . . . . . . . . . . . . . . . . . . . . . . . .

6. . . . . . . . . . . . . . . . . . . . . . . . . . . . . . . . . . . . . . . . . .

7. . . . . . . . . . . . . . . . . . . . . . . . . . . . . . . . . . . . . . . . . .

## DAYS AND MONTHS

A.   What is the first day of the week?      Sunday is the first day. . . . . . . . . . . . . . . . . .

       What is the fifth month of the year? . . . . . . May is the fifth month. . . . . . . . . . .

1. What is the fourth day of the week?    . . . . . . . . . . . . . . . . . . . . . . . . .

2. What is the sixth month of the year?    . . . . . . . . . . . . . . . . . . . . . . . .

3. What is the second day of the week?    . . . . . . . . . . . . . . . . . . . . . . . .

4. What is the tenth month of the year?    . . . . . . . . . . . . . . . . . . . . . . . .

5. What is the twelfth month of the year?    . . . . . . . . . . . . . . . . . . . . . . .

B.   February is the second month of the year.  What can you say about May?

       May is the fifth month of the year.
. . . . . . . . . . . . . . . . . . . . . . . . . . . . . . . . . . . . . . . . . . . . . . . .

1. What can you say about August?

. . . . . . . . . . . . . . . . . . . . . . . . . . . . . . . . . . . . . . . . . . . . . . . .

2. What can you say about November?

. . . . . . . . . . . . . . . . . . . . . . . . . . . . . . . . . . . . . . . . . . . . . . . .

3. What can you say about July?

. . . . . . . . . . . . . . . . . . . . . . . . . . . . . . . . . . . . . . . . . . . . . . . .

4. What can you say about Saturday?

. . . . . . . . . . . . . . . . . . . . . . . . . . . . . . . . . . . . . . . . . . . . . . . .

5. What can you say about Wednesday?

. . . . . . . . . . . . . . . . . . . . . . . . . . . . . . . . . . . . . . . . . . . . . . . .

HAPPY BIRTHDAY!

**A.**      Tom    8/12/60      Tom was born on August 12, 1960. ......................

Mary    6/16/58      Mary was born on June 16, 1958. ......................

1. Bob      3/19/61      .....................................

2. Mike      1/3/47      .....................................

3. Frank      6/8/32      .....................................

4. Judy      8/2/50      .....................................

5. Sally      9/7/47      .....................................

**B.**      Sid      4/13/18

In what month was Sid born?      He was born in April. .................

On what day was he born?      He was born on the thirteenth. ..........

1. Alma      7/20/22

In what year was Alma born?      .............................

On what day was she born?      .............................

2. Steve      2/26/47

On what day was Steve born?      .............................

In what year was he born?      .............................

3. Sue Smith - 10/21/53  (10:30 A.M.)      Sam Smith - 10/21/53  (10:46 A.M.)

In what year were Sam and Sue born? ...........................

What time was Sue born?      .............................

Was Sam or Sue born first?      .............................

How old are they now?      .............................

38                                                                                  Unit Nine

| in | at | on | over | under | to |
|----|----|----|----|----|----|

1. Bob's dog sleeps . . **in** . . . . . . the garage every night.

2. I brush my teeth . . at . . . . night.

3. The lamp is . . . on . . . . the table.

4. Jim was born . . . in . . . . May.

5. I am going . . to . . . . . the store.

6. Please put these books . . in . . . . that box.

7. A bridge is . over . . . . a river.

8. Can you take a vacation . . . in . . . the winter?

9. He put his money . . in . . . . his pocket.

10. Please go with me . . . to . . . . the movies.

11. The show starts . . . . at . . eight o'clock.

12. Jim was born . on . a Monday . in . August . at . six o'clock.

13. Do you like to listen . . . to . . . . . my records?

14. My dog was . under . . the table.

**FIND THE SAME SOUND**

A.

| hungry | puddle | up |
| burn | come | hurry |
| use | touch | jump |
| lunch | month | June |
| us | Tuesday | funny |
| uniform | summer | July |
| chubby | usually | sunny |
| uncle | number | under |

B.

| over | foot | know |
| cold | close | towel |
| top | polish | hope |
| joking | do | stop |
| open | long | hot |
| snow | out | go |
| hotel | jogging | one |
| old | boy | alone |

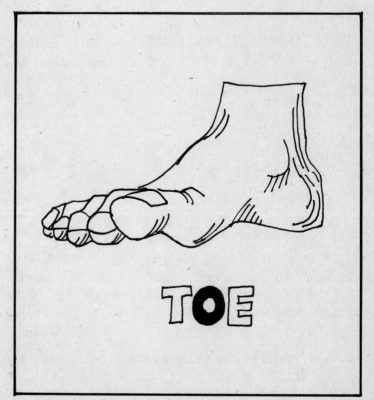

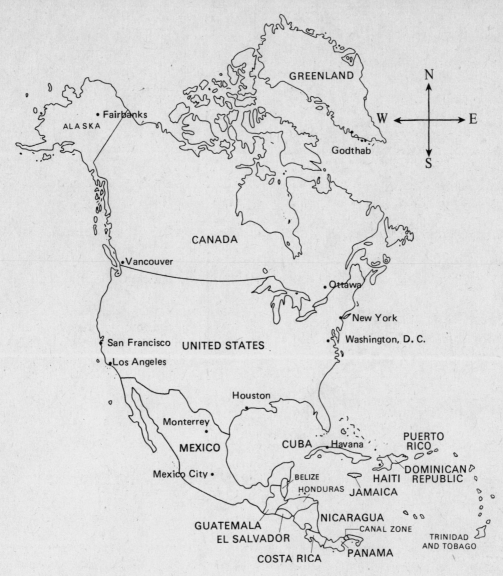

1. Where's Canada?

2. Where's El Salvador?

3. Where's Greenland?

4. Where's Guatemala?

5. Is Monterrey to the north or to the south of Mexico City?

6. Is Washington, D.C. to the north or to the south of New York?

7. Is Los Angeles to the east or to the west of Houston?

8. Is Ottawa to the east or to the west of Vancouver?

**It's north of the United States.**

It's South of the United Stated.

It's north of the united Stated.

It's south of the united Stated.

**It's to the north of Mexico City.**

It's to the South of New York.

It's to the West of Houston.

It's to the east of Vancouver.

# WHOSE IS IT?

**A. Whose hat is this?**    **It's the teacher's.** . . . . . . . . . . . . . . . . . . . . .

1. Whose bread is this?    It's the baby's. . . . . . . . .

2. Whose shoe is this?    It's the grils. . . . . . . . . .

3. Whose jacket is this?    It's the boys. . . . . .

4. Whose boot is this?    It's the waiters. . . . . .

5. Whose plane is this?    It's the pilot's. . . . . . .

**B.**   **Whose car is this?** . . . . . . . . . . . . . . . .   **It's Reynaldo's.**

1. . . . Whose ship is this?    It's Ben's.

2. . . . Whose horse is this?    It's the farmer's.

3. . . . Whose book is this? . . .    It's the teacher's.

4. . . . Whose picture is this? . .    It's Mr. Brown's.

5. . . . Whose radio is this? . .    It's Maria's.

## FIND THE OPPOSITES

| | | | |
|---|---|---|---|
| white | her | seldom | student |
| under | clean | take off | there |
| down | old | hates | full |
| in front of | stand | answer | close |
| last | be born | father | teach |
| go | never | work | die |
| right | bad | thin | feet |
| sunny | south | west | round-trip |

1. ask        answer
2. study      teach
3. here       there
4. play       work
5. open       close
6. him        her
7. often      seldom
8. one-way    round-trip
9. put on     take off
10. likes     hates
11. mother    father
12. live      die
13. always    never
14. sit       stand
15. empty     full
16. behind    in front of

17. over      under
18. black     white
19. up        down
20. first     last
21. come      go
22. teacher   student
23. chubby    thin
24. good      bad
25. dirty     clean
26. new       old
27. hands     feet
28. left      right
29. cloudy    sunny
30. north     south
31. east      west
32. die       be born

## WHAT IS IT?

A.

A school is a place where teachers teach. . . . . . . . . . . . . . . . . . .

1. . . . . . . . . . . . . . . . . . . . . . . . . . . . . . . . . . . . . . . . . . . .

2. . . . . . . . . . . . . . . . . . . . . . . . . . . . . . . . . . . . . . . . . . . .

3. . . . . . . . . . . . . . . . . . . . . . . . . . . . . . . . . . . . . . . . . . . .

4. . . . . . . . . . . . . . . . . . . . . . . . . . . . . . . . . . . . . . . . . . . .

5. . . . . . . . . . . . . . . . . . . . . . . . . . . . . . . . . . . . . . . . . . . .

## WHO IS IT?

B.

A nurse is a person who works in a hospital. . . . . . . . . . . . . . . . . . .

1. . . . . . . . . . . . . . . . . . . . . . . . . . . . . . . . . . . . . . . . . . . .

2. . . . . . . . . . . . . . . . . . . . . . . . . . . . . . . . . . . . . . . . . . . .

3. . . . . . . . . . . . . . . . . . . . . . . . . . . . . . . . . . . . . . . . . . . .

4. . . . . . . . . . . . . . . . . . . . . . . . . . . . . . . . . . . . . . . . . . . .

5. . . . . . . . . . . . . . . . . . . . . . . . . . . . . . . . . . . . . . . . . . . .

Unit Twelve

# FIND THE RIGHT WORD

| | | | |
|---|---|---|---|
| 1. back<br>book<br>bike | 2. same<br>some<br>snow | 3. catch<br>chase<br>crash | 4. tall<br>fall<br>ball |
| 5. state<br>stay<br>start | 6. before<br>beef<br>because | 7. summer<br>sunny<br>some | 8. climb<br>cup<br>clean |
| 9. stand<br>start<br>stop | 10. door<br>floor<br>four | 11. tell<br>tall<br>top | 12. did<br>do<br>dead |
| 13. short<br>shirt<br>skirt | 14. bike<br>bake<br>like | 15. likes<br>legs<br>last | 16. thin<br>time<br>train |
| 17. tape<br>take<br>type | 18. date<br>gate<br>hate | 19. cats<br>catch<br>crash | 20. wave<br>walk<br>wait |
| 21. snow<br>know<br>down | 22. milk<br>mail<br>make | 23. sing<br>ring<br>sigh | 24. boat<br>cook<br>coat |

## TELL A STORY

Pretend you were at a party last night. Tell all about it with these questions.

1. When did the party start?
2. Where was the party?
3. When did you arrive?
4. How many other people were there?
5. What were they doing when you arrived?
6. Your good friend was there. What was he/she wearing?
7. What were you wearing?
8. Did you dance?
9. Did you watch TV?
10. Did you listen to records?
11. Did a boy or girl play the guitar?
12. What did you have to drink?
13. What did you have to eat?
14. Did you walk home?
15. Did you take the bus home?
16. Did your friend take you home?
17. What time did you arrive home?
18. How are you today?
19. What are you going to do tonight?